INTRODUCTION

Over the years I have kept a lot of different kinds of snakes, but one of the first I kept that I considered a real pet was a California Kingsnake. Unlike the wild-caught garter and water snakes from my area, which often adapted well to captivity but were a little too squirmy and

How times have changed! Today, virtually all the Cal Kings you'll see for sale are captive bred. *Herpetoculture,* the science and art of breeding reptiles and amphibians in captivity, has come a long way. Today, many pretty and unusual forms of the California Kingsnake are

Beautiful, hardy, docile, and inexpensive: the California Kingsnake makes an excellent choice for the beginner. Photo by K.H. Switak.

unpredictable to be called pets in the true sense, my first California kingsnake was a docile, beautiful animal, ringed in gold and black. It was calm, never attempted to bite, ever, and lived longer than any other snake I had kept up to that point. It was a wild-caught animal, but it never acted like it.

available, and you'll discover, as I did, that they make fine pets. They are excellent snakes for the beginner who has never kept a snake before. On the other hand, if you have kept snakes before and are ready to move from simply keeping them to breeding them yourself, the Cal King is an excellent subject for your first attempt at snake propagation. Along the way, you'll become interested in other "herps" (shorthand for "reptiles and amphibians" because the science that studies them is *herpetology*), and before you know it you'll have plenty of Cal Kings and other creatures as well. But that's in the future.

WHAT IS A CALIFORNIA KINGSNAKE?

To explain what a California kingsnake is we're going to have to get a bit technical in spots, but I'll talk you through it. We need to look at aspects of both *taxonomy*

Many color and pattern phases of the California Kingsnake are available. Some, like this Hi-yellow King, look so different from the normals that one might think they were a different species altogether. Photo by R.G. Markel.

For now, in this book, my goal is simple. I want you to be able to keep a California Kingsnake or two alive and healthy, and maybe even breed them someday, if you like. But keeping them alive is still my primary goal. Too many herps go to an early grave because their keepers simply didn't know enough about them. Knowledge is power, and I promise that you'll be successful if you follow this book carefully. Along the way, I think it will even be fun!

and *systematics*. Many people, including some scientists who should know better, treat these terms as interchangeable, but they're not. *Taxonomy* refers to the scientific naming of groups of animals, and *systematics* is the science of relationships, or where an animal came from and what its closest relatives are. Ideally, taxonomy is a reflection of the systematics, meaning that the names we choose for animals should reflect their relationships. However, this often is not the

This sharp-looking Desert phase Cal King looks alert and healthy. This is a very popular variety. Photo by I. Francais.

case. Sometimes when an animal is discovered and named we have no idea of its true relationships, or later research shows that our first ideas were wrong. This definitely comes into play with California kingsnakes.

Every animal that is discovered is assigned a scientific ("Latin") name by the person who first describes it, that is, publishes an analysis of how it is different from already named forms. The name consists of two parts, the *genus* and the *species,* and sometimes even a third part, the *subspecies.* The genus has an initial capital letter, and the species is all-lowercase. Both are written in italics or underlined, like so: *Homo sapiens.* That's your (and my) scientific name. To save time and space, once a species is referred to once, its genus may be abbreviated for the rest of the discussion, thus: *H. sapiens.* A species is unique, but a genus may contain many species. All this will get clearer in a moment.

The kingsnakes and milk snakes of the genus *Lampropeltis* are some of the most recognizable snakes from North and Central America, with distinctive colors and patterns that distinguish them from most other snakes. (And as odd as it may look, the tradition is that *kingsnake* is written as one word; *milk snake,* two.) Kingsnakes are members of the family Colubridae, a huge hodgepodge of over 75% of the world's snake species. In fact, the family Colubridae is so diverse that it is probably indefinable,

and herpetologists the world over are working on carving it up into more manageable groupings.

Lampropeltis are distinguished from other North American snakes by smooth, shiny scales, a single anal plate, and many details of their ecology and behavior. The *king* in kingsnake is especially appropriate, as these serpents are renowned for killing and eating other snakes, even venomous ones. Kingsnakes have antigens in their blood that render them immune to all North American pit vipers: copperheads, cottonmouths, and even rattlesnakes! It may seem amazing to consider that the harmless-looking kingsnake is more than a match for the formidable rattlesnake, but it's true. However, many kingsnakes consume even more rodents than reptiles, and they are important predators of the mice and rats we consider vermin.

The California kingsnake is *Lampropeltis getula californiae,* a subspecies of the widespread Common Kingsnake, *L. getula.* The California king is found over almost the entire state of California and also ranges to southern Oregon, south to Baja California, and eastward to southern Nevada, western Arizona, and the southwestern tip of New Mexico. Cal Kings are at home in many different habitats, from sea level to low mountains (5000 feet or less), in deserts, moist coastal forests, and dry upland pine forests.

Interestingly, the California Kingsnake is the only kingsnake

Besides the California Kingsnake, other members of *Lampropeltis* are popular pets. The gorgeous Pueblan Milk Snake, *Lampropeltis triangulum campbelli,* is widely bred and kept. Photo by I. Francais.

that has naturally occurring striped and banded variants. This has had an impact on the snake's taxonomy. The striped form was once considered a full species, *L. californiae,* while the banded phase was considered a subspecies of the Common Kingsnake and named *L. getulus boylii.* In landmark papers in 1936, 1939, and 1944, Lawrence M. Klauber, an amateur herpetologist back in the days when amateur herpetologists still got some respect, proposed and defended the assertion that the striped and banded snakes were mere phases of a single snake, which would have to be called *L. getulus californiae* (the emendation of *getulus* to *getula* occurred in 1988). Klauber, who would later be far more famous for his work with rattlesnakes, backed up his claim by breeding Cal kings and hatching both striped and banded individuals from a single clutch.

VARIETIES

There are currently something on the order of a couple of dozen varieties of the California Kingsnake. Some of these are naturally occurring variants from a particular locality, and some are captive-bred forms that originated as one or a few wild-caught "freaks" that were considered attractive enough to propagate. There is a lot of confusion among herp hobbyists regarding the various *morphs* (forms), especially with regard to propagating them. Some varieties yield offspring of the same variety, while others may produce offspring that look nothing like their parents.

Why is this? There are several reasons. One is that some of the varieties are produced by interactions of several genes, while others are simple one-gene dominant/recessive relationships. Another factor that is often overlooked is the influence of environment on development. In some reptiles, colors and, even more so, color *patterns* can be changed by variables such as the temperature at which the eggs were incubated.

Finally, some of the so-called "morphs" in the hobby are nothing of the sort. A morph should be a variety of fairly consistent appearance that can reproduce others of its type. Some just don't do that. Some breeding lines will throw a lot of "oddities," and if you breed hundreds or

This California Kingsnake serves as an example of the typical Banded phase. This is probably the most common and inexpensive variety. Photo by S. Kochetov.

Striped Albino California Kingsnakes are beautiful and popular. However, some keepers report the albino varieties tend to be more high-strung than normally colored snakes. Photo by W.P. Mara

thousands of baby snakes, you may be able to cherry-pick individuals with a similar oddity from among them. Just because two snakes look similar does not necessarily mean that they're related, or that the same gene and/or environmental condition produced them.

One of the most used and abused terms in herpetoculture is "hetero," which is short for *heterozygous*. A heterozygous animal is one that has a hidden gene for a particular recessive trait. For instance, if you breed a genetically pure normal snake to a genetically pure albino one (these are called *homozygous*), all the offspring will be heterozygous. They will all look normal, but they will be carrying (and not showing) the recessive gene for albinism. If you breed two of the heteros to each other, or cross it to a pure albino, some of the offspring will be albino. So, if you buy a Cal King that's sold as "hetero for albino," what the breeder is really telling you is that even though the snake looks normal, if you grow the snake out and breed it to another hetero or albino, you'll get some albino offspring. This can be a relatively cheap way to get a desirable variety (eventually). For instance, albino milk snakes are some of the most sought-after snakes in the hobby today, but it'll set you back a thousand dollars or more to buy one; the heteros, however, are cheaper. However, you'll have to invest several years in growing them to maturity, and only then will you know if your investment was worth it. That's because the "hetero" label is a great way for an unscrupulous breeder to make a few extra bucks on a normal snake. It's a bit like a used car salesman saying, "Yeah, I know it looks like a Gremlin, but under the hood it's really a Cadillac!"

I don't want to overemphasize this bit. In my experience, most herp breeders are pretty conscientious about their product, but let the buyer beware! Fortunately, with regard to Cal Kings, the albinos sell for only a little bit more than the normals to begin with; however, snakes that are hetero for some of the other colors or patterns listed below may be more expensive. If I were you, I'd spend the extra money and buy a snake that actually showed the trait you desire, not one with the trait allegedly buried somewhere in its genes.

Now we'll take a very quick look at some of the varieties of Cal Kings. This is by no means an exhaustive list, because breeders are constantly creating new varieties, often by combining the existing ones. For instance, if there's a purple morph and a polka-dotted morph, you can bet that someone's already working on the purple-polka-dotted morph.

By the way, the terms *morph, variety, phase,* and *form* are used interchangeably. Don't get too

Crisp white markings are the hallmarks of the Desert phase California Kingsnake. This one was photographed in southern California. Photo by K.H. Switak.

attached to one over the other, because the breeders are not consistent in their usage of the terms, and in the discussions below I will be jumping back and forth between them as well.

BANDED

The most familiar phase of the California Kingsnake is the form once known as *Lampropeltis*

rather than *banded* because the pattern continues ventrally. The lower part of the head is also light in color, particularly the labials (lip scales).

STRIPED

Once considered a full species, *Lampropeltis californiae*, the "true" California King has an unbroken, narrow (about 1.5-2

Desert phase California Kingsnakes can be banded or striped, like this one. This hatchling has a completely unbroken stripe, a desired rarity. Photo by W. P. Mara.

getulus boylii, or the Pacific Kingsnake. It is usually a dark brown to blackish snake with whitish-yellow bands about 2-3 scales wide, thinner dorsally and wider ventrally. The light bands widen even more and continue across the belly; the dark bands also continue ventrally. It is really better to call these snakes *ringed*

scale rows wide) white-yellow dorsal stripe. The several lowermost scale rows often are at least partially yellow or white, and the belly is without banding but may be either light or dark, with some mottling of the reverse color. Facial scales are light-colored, and there is often a light spot on the nape of the head.

ALBINO

Technically, albinism is the absence of the black pigment *melanin*. Other pigments may still be present, however. In Cal kings, both striped and banded forms are available as albinos, and in these the bands or stripes are bright yellow. The rest of the body

amelanistic, to underscore the fact that the black color is the only one that's lacking.

SNOW

There is, however, a truly patternless, pinkish-white albino form of the Cal King, and the few breeders producing it usually refer

Breeding for larger bands of white has resulted in 50/50 Desert phase snakes. These are strikingly beautiful snakes, as can be seen here. Photo by I. Francais.

is light pink, and the eyes are bright ruby-red because the lack of pigment allows the color of the blood vessels in the retina to shine through. Because typical albino Cal Kings have at least some yellow color, and because most people think of albinos as white, patternless animals, some prefer to call these snakes

to it as the "snow" morph. Both albinos are simple recessives, meaning that the normal color will dominate if you cross an albino with a fully pigmented snake. If you want more albinos, simply breed albino-to-albino, preferably of the same bloodline. Snow X amelanistic crosses are less predictable.

Hi-yellow Cal Kings are the results of many generations of selective breeding. They are steps along the path to a pure yellow Cal King, which has still eluded breeders. Photo by P. Freed.

HYPOMELANISTIC

There is yet a third type of "albino" in the California Kingsnake: the hypomelanistic or "lavender" phase. This is a snake with reduced melanin (the prefix *hypo* means "less" or "reduced"), but it is not entirely absent. These snakes tend to look like "dirty" amelanistics. The skin has a heavy patina of lavender or light gray. As these snakes grow they usually lose the lavender coloration and become normal but light-colored (chocolate, etc.) adults.

Lavender Cal Kings have reduced amounts of melanin in their skin. Since melanin is not totally absent, their eyes are pigmented unlike those of true albinos. Photo by I. Francais.

This oddly patterned snake is typical of the Cal Kings found in the Long Beach and Newport areas of California. Note the broken bands and extensively yellow sides. Photo by L. G. Markel.

DESERT

The "desert phase" of the Cal King is typified by deep, shiny black and ice-white colors, with no mixing of the two. These are exceptionally handsome and prized serpents. Desert Cal Kings can be striped or banded, the banded being somewhat more common. Snakes of this description *tend* to come from the part of the Mojave desert in Southern California and adjacent Arizona, but they may appear in the other populations as well. There is a tendency in the trade to label any Cal king with a crisp black-and-white pattern as a "desert," regardless of where its ancestors originated.

50/50

Often called "50/50 desert," these are snakes with unusually wide light bands, to the point that they are roughly 50% black and 50% white. Ideal specimens are very clean-looking, like an ideal desert phase, because they have no light tipping of the dark scales or vice versa.

CHOCOLATE

Also known as the coastal or Pacific morph, Cal kings from coastal California tend to have a ground color that is a rich chocolate-brown, very distinct from the black of the "desert" type. The light bands or stripes are cream to bright yellow.

LONG BEACH/NEWPORT

Named for the region of California where they are most often found, these snakes have a yellow dorsal stripe and a great deal this color on the flanks,

Coastal or Chocolate phase snakes have a dark brown coloration. They are typically, but not necessarily, from stock captured near the California coast. Photo by K. Lucas.

interspersed with dots, dashes, stripes, or zigzags of the (usually) chocolate ground color. Long Beach/Newport kings are incredibly variable, but some of them are very attractive snakes with over 50% light color.

spotting on or between the scales and a black blotch or pair of blotches behind the head. To the best of my knowledge no one has yet produced a 100% pure yellow Cal King, though many breeders are working toward this goal.

The Cal Kings from Baja tend to be darkly colored melanistic snakes. These were formerly recognized as the subspecies *conjuncta*. These are often sold by breeders as Baja Kings. Photo by R.G. Markel.

HI-YELLOW

Breeders working mostly with Long Beach/Newport animals have increased the yellow even further in some bloodlines. Often sold are "75% yellow" and the even more prized (need I mention they're also more expensive?) "90%+ yellow." The latter are sometimes called "banana," and are almost entirely yellow, with only a little bit of black edging or

YUMA

Some of the kings from southeastern California and southwestern Arizona have a dark gray ground color and narrow light bands. In addition, the light scales often have dark edging, the effect of which is to make the light bands look muted. This was once considered a valid subspecies, *L. getula yumensis*, but today herpetologists consider it merely another of the myriad variations of *L. g. californiae.* However, the last word may not yet be written on this form, as some believe it is really an intergrade (subspecific hybrid) between the California Kingsnake and the Desert Kingsnake, *L. g. splendida.* DNA analysis would probably confirm whether there is genetic material from both of these subspecies in the Yuma Kingsnake, but so far it is a mystery.

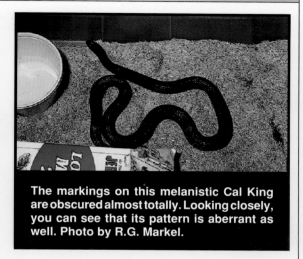

The markings on this melanistic Cal King are obscured almost totally. Looking closely, you can see that its pattern is aberrant as well. Photo by R.G. Markel.

BROAD-STRIPE

Striped-phase Cal Kings with unusually wide dorsal stripes, more than three scale rows, are called wide- or broad-stripes. Most of these originated from the vicinity of Carlsbad, California.

BROKEN-STRIPE

Striped-phase snakes show a strong tendency toward breaks in the dorsal stripe, especially on the tail. Most breeders and hobbyists prefer that the dorsal stripe in a striped-phase Cal King is complete and unbroken, but if the breaks are many and regular they can produce an attractive pattern of dots or dashes.

REVERSE-STRIPE

Some hi-yellow individuals have a sort of reversed pattern, with a more or less yellow ground color and a black dorsal stripe. While a yellow snake with a black stripe would probably be pretty, reverse stripes are not quite there yet. The dorsal stripe is always broken, and there are often secondary dashes adjacent to it.

MELANISTIC

Melanism is the opposite of albinism. Melanistic snakes have an overabundance of black, to the point that it may totally obscure other patterning. From the tip of Baja California are two melanistic forms of the California Kingsnake that were once considered separate subspecies, *L. g. conjuncta* (a banded form) and *L. g. nitida* (striped). Extreme forms of *"nitida"* in particular are handsome, solid black snakes. Melanistic individuals may pop up in any population of Cal Kings, but in the Baja populations it is a normal tendency rather than a freakish occurrence.

GHOST

I think a better name for this variety would be "clouded." Specimens tend to be grayish, with no distinct stripes or bands of cream, but with the light color instead in irregular, fuzzy patches.

ABERRANT

This is a catch-all "phase" for almost anything that can't be pigeonholed into one of the other varieties, but the term tends to refer more to oddities of pattern than of color. Snakes with zigzags, blotches, light bands with dark centers, and wavy patterns are among those that are traded as aberrants. The unfortunate thing is that every one of these is probably unique, and you couldn't produce more just like it if you tried.

SELECTING AND HANDLING

Selecting a healthy Cal King is relatively easy. Examine the snake for any signs of injury. Visible scars are signs that the snake has not been handled well, so beware. However, even more telling are any unhealed wounds. Such a snake should immediately be disqualified from consideration. Look for signs of mites at the edges of the scales; they look a bit like finely ground paprika. Often the feces of mites are more apparent than the mites themselves; the feces show up as silvery-gray dust. The snake should have a full look; skinny

Besides the California Kingsnake, most other subspecies of the Common Kingsnake are readily available. This is the Mexican Black Kingsnake, *L. g. nigrita*. Photo by R. G. Markel.

snakes would be somewhat triangular in cross section, and the ridge of the backbone would be clearly visible. In addition, a skinny snake would show clear bone outlines just under the skin at the nape of the neck. Malnourished snakes are also to be avoided. Check the mouth and pass if the snake has any runny or cheesy material at the margins of the mouth. If there are any relatively fresh stools in the snake's cage, they should be firm, not runny, and free of slime or blood. In addition, a snake should be alert and responsive.

Cal Kings almost always are gentle snakes, but always handle one before purchasing to determine this. There is some individual variation in temperament, and a rare few will be completely intractable. I'll never forget one particularly vicious striped albino I had; it could never be handled without biting savagely. It helps if you feed your snake(s) in a separate enclosure from their home cage. That way, they don't become conditioned into thinking that every time you open their cage it's feeding time and thus time to bite at anything that moves, i.e., you.

The gorgeous Desert Kingsnake, *L. g. splendida*, ranges over the southwestern U. S. and northern Mexico. Desert Kings tend to be less available than some other subspecies. Photo by R.G. Markel.

Often called the Chain or Chainlink Kingsnake, the Eastern King, *L. g. getula,* ranges from New Jersey south to Florida. It is the largest of the kingsnakes, occasionally reaching 6.5 feet in length. Photo by K.H. Switak.

HOUSING

California Kingsnakes are easy to house, and do not take up an inordinate amount of room in your home. I often wonder why people keep huge snakes such as Burmese Pythons, because in the same space it takes to house one adult python you could keep a large breeding colony of Cal Kings! In addition, that colony of Cal Kings will cost far less to feed than a behemoth of a python. Different strokes for different folks, I guess. (You python people, *don't* write me nasty letters! I'm sure your snakes are lovely. But, I'm glad they're in your home and not mine. I don't have the room or the money.)

CONTAINERS

Cal Kings can be kept in a wide variety of different types and sizes of containers. All-glass aquariums (minus the water, of course!) are going to be the cages employed by most of us because they are relatively inexpensive and easy to deal with. Hatchlings can be kept in tanks as small as 5 gallons; juveniles, 10-gallon tanks; adults should be housed in 20-gallon "long" tanks (which are 30 inches long). All tanks should have a tight-fitting screen top with a grid of metal hardware cloth.

Some keepers need lighter and more efficient containers. This especially applies to those who

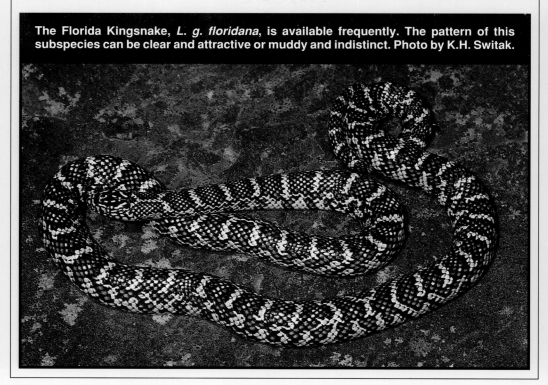

The Florida Kingsnake, *L. g. floridana*, is available frequently. The pattern of this subspecies can be clear and attractive or muddy and indistinct. Photo by K.H. Switak.

This Cal King has an aberrant pattern that appears to be a fusion of the Banded and Striped phases. This could be a genetic trait or the result of environmental influences during development. Photo by W.P. Mara.

keep breeding groups and/or large numbers of juveniles and need cages that can be easily stacked or shelved. Plastic sweater and shoe boxes are often used, but there are even better, more transparent plastic boxes on the market today that are designed especially for the purpose (though herp breeders still call them "sweater boxes" and "shoeboxes" out of habit).

SUBSTRATES

Few subjects provoke more controversy among herp people than the type of flooring—the *substrate*—to use in a reptile cage. There are several available to you, and each one has advantages and disadvantages.

Sand is my personal favorite. It's attractive, very natural-looking (especially if you're keeping desert-phase Cal Kings), cheap, and easily replaced. Fecal material dries out readily on sand, so sand is not especially conducive to bacterial and fungal growth, and that's good. Moist substrates encourage the latter, and often lead to skin diseases in snakes. On the other hand, some sand will invariably be ingested when the snakes are fed. Excessive sand in the gut can form concrete-like gut impactions, and there is no doubt that this has led to the deaths of reptiles. I've seen the X-rays, so I can't say that this never happens. However, I will say that it *rarely* happens,

Speckled Kingsnakes, *L. g. holbrooki*, are always pretty snakes. They occur over a wide range in the U.S., and western individuals often resemble Desert Kings. Speckled Kings are very frequently bred. Photo by M. Burger.

and when it does I feel that there are probably other circumstances at play too. As long as you use a fine grade of clean silica sand, remove all fecal material promptly along with a generous scoop of sand from the surrounding area, and replace *all* the sand twice a year, I believe you have nothing to worry about. Also, feed the snake in such a way as to minimize the ingestion of sand, such as feeding it in a separate container or putting the food on a rock.

Gravel should be avoided, in my opinion. The large pore spaces let waste matter penetrate into nooks and crannies where it can fester, and gravel holds far more moisture than sand. Small bark chips are okay as a substrate. Pine mulch or orchid bark mulch are fine. Do not use cedar chips, which contain aromatic oils that are irritating to reptiles, if not downright toxic. Avoid topsoil or potting soil.

Many people use newspaper as a reptile bedding. I think it's awfully ugly, but it is very cheap, very functional, and very easy to change. It dries quickly. Some people are concerned that the ink in the paper may be toxic, but this probably isn't true. In almost all cases these days newspapers and magazines are printed with soy-based, nontoxic inks. For the benefit of the doubt, don't use colored newspaper (the Sunday funnies, for instance), but any black & white paper should be okay. If you're still leery, white paper towels are a little more expensive but just as good.

Astroturf is seen with some frequency as a reptile substrate. The idea is that it's nearly

L. g. nigra, the "other" Black Kingsnake. This subspecies of Illinois south to Alabama retains more yellow than the Mexican Black Kingsnake. It is not frequently bred. Photo by G. Carlzen.

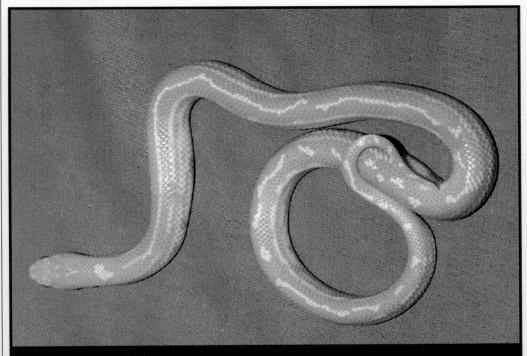

Here is a wonderful example of a Broken-stripe Albino Cal King. Often, individuals like these show up in clutches accidentally, as most breeders select for snakes with unbroken stripes. Photo by W.P. Mara.

indestructible, so when it gets soiled you can hose it off, dry it, and use it again. In reality, it is hard to get this stuff completely clean, and simply washing it may not be enough. Boiling it might be, but who has that kind of time? Additionally, the stuff is pretty abrasive (ask a pro linebacker how he feels about artificial turf!), so I am concerned that snakes might scrape themselves raw on it, and possibly get the wounds infected if the turf isn't clean.

The final choice of substrate depends mostly on your esthetic preferences and your budget. No matter what you use, think *clean!* Use something you can either discard or clean very thoroughly.

LIGHT AND HEAT

Snakes are reptiles, which means that they're what most people call "cold-blooded." This actually is not the most accurate term we could use, because a snake can have a body temperature very close to your own. What we really mean is that a snake's body temperature is dependent on its environment. They don't generate heat internally like mammals and birds. On the other hand, keeping your body at 98.6°F all the time takes a *lot* of energy, meaning food. Snakes and other reptiles don't use their food to warm their bodies, but instead get it for free from the environment, by basking in the sun or curling up on a

Attractive shelving units like these recently have become more available at pet stores and reptile shows. Some come with built-in heating tape or pads. Photo by I. Francais.

the time and they're not. They have just evolved different solutions to the problems of energy regulation that all living creatures have to deal with.

Reptiles are what we call *behavioral thermoregulators;* they shuttle back and forth between warm and cool places and thus maintain a reasonably constant body temperature. We can help them do this in captivity by making sure their cage has a *thermal gradient.* This just means that one end of the cage is warm, the other end is cool, and the temperature changes fairly evenly over the length in between.

To do this, place an incandescent spotlight (60 to 75 watts is usually plenty) over one corner of the cage. A note of caution: never place the light inside the cage. A snake may curl up directly on top of it and burn itself severely or fatally, to say

warm rock. There are trade-offs. For instance, a snake can only be active when it's warm outside; a mammal like you can be active anytime. On the other hand, a snake needs far less food than a mammal of equal size, so it doesn't need to be ready for action all the time. So don't consider snakes to be "primitive" animals because you're warm-blooded all nothing of the fire hazard this creates. The light must be outside the cage, above the wire mesh top. Directly below and inside the cage should be a large flat rock or sturdy wooden bough. This will be the basking site for your snake. Aim the spotlight at the basking site and measure the air

retiring to the hide box when it feels warm, or even laying somewhere in between to maintain an intermediate temperature.

Some keepers of Cal kings use "hot rocks" to provide heat for their snakes. These are electrically heated plaster or

Many keepers use shredded aspen as the substrate for their Cal Kings. Aspen is generally regarded as safer for reptiles than pine or cedar. Photo by I. Francais.

temperature about an inch above it. Ideally, it will be about 80-86°F. You may have to move the spotlight up or down until you get the right temperature.

The opposite end of the cage will be cooler, likely by about 10°F or so. This is where you should place the snake's hide box. Now, your snake can regulate its own temperature by moving to the basking site when it feels cold and

ceramic "stones." I would use these with care. I have seen hot rocks get way too hot and burn the bellies of reptiles that laid on them. I would only use them if they had thermostatic controls (costs more but is worth it), and even then my tendency would be to bury a hot rock in the sand so that the snake couldn't touch it directly. This would also diffuse the heat over a wider area. Make sure that you carefully read the manufacturer's directions for a hot rock so that you do nothing with it that could create a fire hazard. Perhaps the best usage for a hot rock is to provide nighttime heat if the cage is in a cool room. The cage light and hot rock can be put on timers so that the light comes on during the day and the hot rock switches on about an hour after "sunset" and off again about an hour before "sunrise." It may take a little bit of fine-tuning, but you should have no trouble using lights and/or hot rocks to create a stable thermal gradient for your snake. An undertank heating pad is probably a better option than a hot rock.

Full-spectrum lighting to provide UV radiation (which aids in vitamin D synthesis and calcium metabolism) can be provided, but I don't believe it's necessary in this case. I don't think Cal Kings spend enough time basking for it to make a difference. It's better to provide regular vitamin/mineral supplementation with your snake's food.

Finally, I should mention that the housing layout I've been describing is for one snake in a display cage. Some people, especially breeders, maintain large numbers of Cal kings and have to do it as efficiently as possible. They omit the self-contained lighting and heating systems and maintain the snakes in 10-gallon aquaria or large sweater boxes that can be placed into a bookshelf-like arrangement with heat tapes running underneath the shelves, toward the rear, creating a gentle thermal gradient from the front to the back of each shelf. The individual cages just slide in in modular fashion. Each one is provided with just a water bowl, a simple hide box, and an easily removed substrate such as newspaper or paper towels.

Cal Kings do not climb as avidly as the rat snakes, but they will climb on branches and rocks occasionally. Also, the roughness of wood can help them shed. Photo by I. Francais.

Cleanliness is one of the most important factors in keeping your Cal King healthy. The water bowl can be a major source of bacteria if not cleaned daily. Photo by I. Francais.

FEEDING

California kings generally are not difficult snakes to feed. Most captives will regularly eat appropriately sized rodents, though a few newborns will need some coaxing. California kingsnakes are *constrictors,* and no, that doesn't mean they're related to boa constrictors. The term refers to a method that some snakes use to kill their prey, and by coincidence kingsnakes and boas (and pythons, and rat snakes, and a host of others) happen to share it. Snakes that kill by constriction wrap coils of their body around a prey animal and progressively tighten. Contrary to popular belief, they do not crush their prey, but prevent the prey from breathing until it suffocates. Every time the prey exhales, the snake tightens its coils a bit more, until finally it's impossible for the prey to expand its chest to take a breath. In the case of a rodent, constriction often kills in less than a minute. It sounds gruesome, but it is a remarkably quick and efficient method of predation.

Fortunately for squeamish keepers, as well as for the snakes, it usually is not necessary to offer your snakes live rodents. Frozen mice and rats in many sizes are available, by the piece or in bulk, and most Cal Kings will readily

Never house Cal Kings with other snakes, including other Cal Kings. You may end up with one fat Cal King. This Cal King is eating a Gopher Snake, *Pituophis catenifer.* Photo by K.H. Switak.

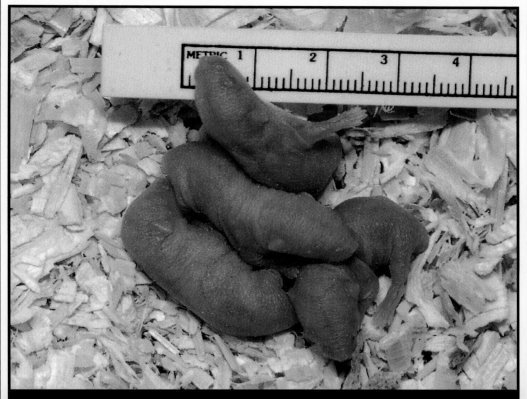

Pinky mice, live or frozen, are the staple diet of hatchling Cal Kings. Always be careful not to feed snakes food that is too big for them. Photo by M. & J. Walls.

take them. I highly recommend that you *NOT* feed live rodents to your snakes unless absolutely necessary, especially not adult rodents. Mice often do not "go gently into that good night," and bite and scratch at their attacker. If the snake does not have a firm grip on them from the first strike, they can sometimes turn the tables, and have been known to maim or even kill snakes. It is especially dangerous to leave a live mouse overnight in the cage with a snake that does not seem interested in feeding. Many a keeper has awakened to find a prized snake dead or bleeding from multiple bites.

By the way, don't thaw your feeder rodents in the microwave; they have a tendency to explode! Instead, put them in a cup of hot water for 10 or 15 minutes, blot them dry, and offer them to your snake(s).

MICE

Most Cal kings will feed well for their entire lives on mice of one size or another. Herp keepers generally refer to mice according to four size categories. *Pinkies* are tiny newborn mice, pink and hairless, under an inch long, with eyes closed and only capable of squirming movements. *Fuzzies* are several days to a week older,

A beautiful hatchling Striped Albino Cal King. Most Cal Kings retain their bright colors as they age. Photo by J. Merli.

and inch long or slightly larger, and are starting to show some fur and whiskers; they can crawl a bit, but their eyes are still closed. *Hoppers* are bigger still, about 1.5 inches long; they have disproportionately large heads but are well-furred, able to walk, and their eyes are beginning to open. *Adult* mice are about three to four inches long, not counting tail. Obviously, these divisions are somewhat artificial because there is a whole range of intermediate sizes.

With regard to using mice as snake food, there are several important nutritional facts to remember. Pinkies and fuzzies are higher in fat than older mice, and they are not a particularly good source of calcium because their bones are not yet well-developed. Smaller snakes need these young mice as food, but they should always have their rumps dipped in a vitamin/mineral supplement. These supplements are particularly important for supplying the Vitamin D3 and calcium that young snakes require for their growing bones and that breeding adult females require for depositing healthy shells on their eggs.

RATS

Some individual snakes can be a bit reluctant to take mice, and so an option is to offer "rat pups." These are essentially rat fuzzies, three or four weeks old, but they

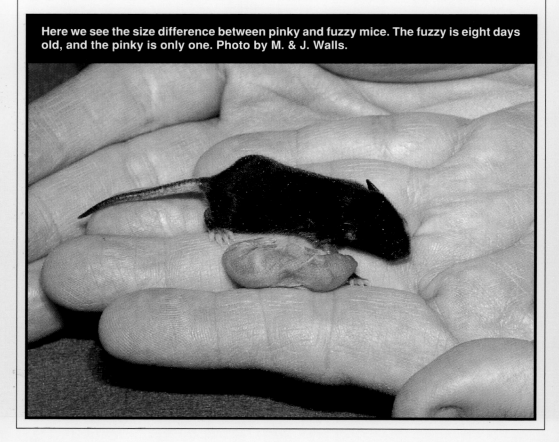

Here we see the size difference between pinky and fuzzy mice. The fuzzy is eight days old, and the pinky is only one. Photo by M. & J. Walls.

Generally speaking, feeding your Cal King will not be a problem; moreso, you will need to be careful not to overfeed the snake. Photo by I. Francais.

Kingsnakes are famous for eating other snakes. Above: **A Cal King wraps around a Leaf-nosed Snake,** *Phyllorhynchus decurtatus,* **constricting the snake like it would mammalian prey.** Below: **After the prey is dead, it is swallowed head first. Kingsnakes can swallow snakes that are nearly as large as themselves. Photos by K.H. Switak.**

In the wild, lizards form a large part of the diet of the California Kingsnakes, especially the young snakes. This Striped Cal King is devouring a Western Banded Gecko, *Coleonyx variegatus.* Photo by K.H. Switak.

weigh about a much as a young adult mouse. Why some snakes like these better than mice is a bit of a mystery to me, but it happens. Perhaps it's the scent. Having kept both, I can confirm that rats do smell different from mice, though I can't describe exactly how. They both smell kind of musky, not really unpleasant once you get used to them, but they don't smell the same. Just as we humans have our favorite foods, snakes also have individual preferences.

LIZARDS

In the wild, lizards and small snakes form part of a California King's diet, but offering them in captivity is not recommended because of the risk of transferring reptilian pathogens from prey to predator. For a relative few young snakes some reptilian prey may be necessary to get them eating, but it's best to wean them onto rodents at the earliest opportunity. See the section on rearing the young in the "Breeding" chapter for more details.

WATER

Clean fresh water must be supplied *daily,* in bowls just a bit too small for the snakes to curl up and soak in, which they should not be encouraged to do for risk of chilling and respiratory infection. Wash the water bowls with scalding water, and use a bit of

Above: **To encourage a reluctant eater, you can try putting the snake and prey in a small, closed container for a few hours. Make sure the prey is dead or otherwise not a threat to the snake.** Photo by W.P. Mara. Below: **Most Cal Kings will take mice, frozen or live, without a problem.** Photo by I. Francais.

The Side-blotched Lizard, *Uta stansburiana,* is a small U.S. lizard that is sometimes sold as a feeder lizard. Photo by A. Norman.

baking soda with a sponge as an abrasive to remove any waste matter. Occasionally a snake will defecate in its water dish (some of them just have no class!), and it is vital to sterilize the bowls with bleach before reusing them.

FEEDING FREQUENCY

In most cases Cal Kings should be fed about once a week, with an average of about two rodents appropriate to their size. Hatchlings should be fed more frequently, about three feedings, one pinkie mouse per feeding. Feedings should be accelerated at certain times of the year: just before and after hibernation/ brumation, and during the breeding season.

Rat pups at two days and two weeks old. If your Cal King seems to dislike mice, you can try rat pups. Adult rats, however, are too big for even the largest Cal Kings. Photo by N. Mays.

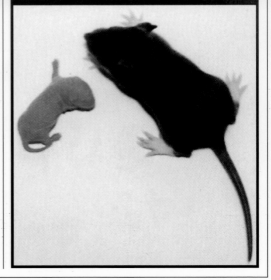

BREEDING

The California Kingsnake is a relatively easy snake to breed. In fact, it may well be the easiest of the colubrids to propagate, with the possible exception of the Corn Snake (*Elaphe guttata*). Some have gone so far as to call the Corn Snake the first fully domesticated reptile, but I say that the Cal King isn't far behind. Breeders vary in their methods, but I'll outline a basic breeding program below and do my best to let you know where there are "options."

SEXING

It goes without saying that the first step in breeding Cal Kings is to actually get a pair. Sexed adult pairs are sometimes seen for sale, but it is probably better to get a couple of young snakes and grow them out. I tend to be the suspicious type, and if a breeder is getting rid of an adult pair, I'd want to know why. A healthy pair has the potential to produce up to several dozen young a year, so most breeders won't give up the that income. A very large pair *may* be old snakes that are reproductively spent. In the long run, I think you'll be happier with young snakes you raise yourself. When they eventually breed—and they will—you'll definitely feel a greater sense of accomplishment.

There are about three ways to sex Cal Kings. One way is to simply look at the underside of

Female kingsnakes will usually lay their eggs in damp sphagnum moss without a problem. For the best hatching results, the eggs must be placed in an incubator. Photo by I. Francais.

Quite a few breeders mate the different subspecies together. This can create some attractive snakes, like this Desert King/Cal King intergrade, but the practice is widely disdained, as it produces "mutts." Photo by R.G. Markel.

the tail below the anal plate. You'll need to look at a group of snakes for this, because you can only do this by comparison. The tail of a male is relatively longer and heavier than that of a female and is slightly swollen below the base because of the presence of the *hemipenis.* In all snakes and lizards the hemipenis of the male is a two-lobed structure, often equipped with ridges and hooks that help it stay attached to the female long enough for sperm transfer to take place. Normally, only one lobe is inserted into the female's cloaca; it doesn't matter which. When not mating, the hemipenis is turned inside-out and retracted into pouches at the base of the tail, and this is what makes the male's tail stouter than the female's. The female's tail is noticeably longer and has a more even taper.

This method of sexing works okay, but there are a number of things that can throw it off. First, you should ideally compare snakes of exactly the same size and age. How well the snakes have been feeding can also introduce a doubt factor. For instance, a very well-fed female will have extra fat deposited in the tail that could make it look thicker and cause you to mistake her for a male. The comparison method works reasonably well if you have a number of snakes to work with, and has the advantage of being completely non-intrusive. However, if making a mistake is going to be a big deal to you, get someone to help you with one of the following two methods.

The second method is *popping.* This works only with hatchlings or small juveniles. On large snakes this method no longer

The long-awaited sight: Cal Kings hatching. Breeding Cal Kings is not especially difficult, but you should gather as much information as you can before trying it. Photo by W.P. Mara.

works, and can cause serious injury. Simply put, by squeezing gently on both sides of the base of the tail it is possible to pop out the hemipenis of a male snake. If the snake is a female, nothing happens. Please don't try this yourself until someone experienced shows you the right touch. It is very easy to squeeze too hard and damage a snake, especially a female. When the hemipenis doesn't pop you might say to yourself, "So, is this a female, or am I not squeezing hard enough? Maybe I'll squeeze a little harder...." Bad idea.

The third method is *probing*. A small, blunt-ended stainless steel surgical probe is coated with petroleum jelly or a similar sterile lubricant and inserted into the cloaca of the snake very gently and worked posteriorly (toward the tail tip) and slightly to one side. If the snake is a female, the probe will enter one of the pheromone-producing scent pouches, which are quite shallow. In a male the probe enters a lobe of the inverted hemipenis, which lies inside a much deeper pouch. As with the previous method, it is very easy to damage or even kill the snake if you don't know what you're doing. You really must have an experienced snake person show you the right way to probe a snake. I can only describe it here; I can't reach out of the book and show you exactly the right amount of pressure to use. Both probing and popping are easy once you get the hang of them, but experience is the key.

HIBERNATION

Okay. For the sake of discussion let's say it's two years later. During that time you've fed your pair of snakes generously, and they are now at least 36 inches long. They are now sexually mature. Two years is the average length of time it takes to get Cal kings to maturity. It is possible to get them reproducing at 18 months or even a little bit earlier by stuffing them with food from day one, but I don't recommend it. Some breeders believe that reptiles forced to breed at an early age "burn out" sooner than those that aren't, living shortened lives or at least shortened *reproductive* lives. Better to be safe than sorry. Besides, I'm making the assumption that someone reading this book is not going to get into large-scale commercial breeding right off the bat. If you have only a pair or two of snakes, be patient. You'll get plenty of young out of them over the long haul.

Although there are exceptions, Cal Kings almost always must have a winter rest before they can be bred. Some call this *hibernation,* but these snakes don't really hibernate in the true sense, which means becoming completely inactive for several months or more and never rousing from a coma-like sleep. Winter inactivity in most North American snakes, including Cal Kings, is more correctly called *brumation.* In brumation, a snake is torpid most of the time, but if the weather gets unseasonably warm the snake may sluggishly make its way out of the den for a short time. Even when the weather does not change, the snake will periodically change position inside the den.

Preparing pet kingsnakes for brumation is not difficult. In late summer and early autumn, feed the snakes a *lot!* Two or three adult mice a week is about right. If kept up for a long time this would result in a seriously obese snake, but you want the snake to build up its fat stores before brumation. In early November (assuming you live in the Northern Hemisphere), stop feeding, but continue to supply plenty of water. Keep lighting and temperature at normal levels. After about two weeks the snakes' intestinal tracts should be empty of fecal matter and undigested food. Now you can begin to reduce the temperature and photoperiod (day length). Over the course of two more weeks, cut back the photoperiod to about 8 hours and turn the heat down and finally off, so that the temperature is steady in the mid-50s Fahrenheit. Each snake should be brumated individually. Continue to provide fresh, clean water on a regular basis, as the snakes will occasionally wake up for long enough to take a drink. If your follow the schedule, your snakes will be down for the winter on about the first of December.

I'll mention here that some breeders believe it's not necessary to take temperature and photoperiod manipulation to extremes mentioned above. Some simply cool the snakes to about 65°F and keep them in the dark most of the time, but do not become so obsessive about it that they won't turn on the lights and check the snakes every week or so. Other breeders are very serious about photoperiod/ temperature manipulation and claim they get better yields at breeding time. Take your pick...both methods will work. If you get serious enough to be concerned about maximizing production from your breeders, you can conduct your own experiments to see what works best for you.

How long to keep the snakes in brumation is also a matter of some disagreement, with some breeders keeping them down for only eight weeks or so, others 12 to 14 weeks.

Why are we going to all this trouble? First of all, the snakes simply need the rest after seven or eight months of continuous activity, especially if they bred that year. Brumation lets the snakes "recharge their batteries," especially with regard to hormone levels. In male snakes, sperm production and testosterone levels are highest in the spring and taper off afterward. If he is not rested during the winter, his sperm count will remain low the following spring, and even if he can become aroused enough to mate (not easy with low testosterone), he probably will not be very fertile, perhaps being totally infertile. Females will have few if any ovarian follicles (the precursors of eggs) in a state of readiness, and will not be very receptive to the males. In short, if you don't brumate your snakes, they probably won't be very willing to mate, and, even if they do, you probably will get few or no fertile eggs out of them.

Once the snakes are active, make sure they are healthy. Look for any signs of bubbly mucus around the mouth that might indicate a respiratory infection. Any snake that shows odd

These hatchlings are a mixed group. Some appear to be Hi-yellow while others are Banded. It is not rare to get some variation within the same clutch. Photo by R.G. Markel.

MATING

In early to mid-March it's time to rouse the snakes. Basically, just reverse the sequence you followed during the cool-down period—over two weeks, return photoperiod and temperature to normal. Here's another area where some breeders do it quick & dirty and do just fine. They simply turn on the lights and crank up the heat, and within a day or two the snakes are up and around. I recommend taking a little more time.

symptoms should be rushed off to your reptile vet. (Yes, you really should have one. More on that later.)

Continue to keep the sexes separated for now, and get them feeding. They will be hungry and eager to eat, and the temptation will be to feed them a big meal right away. Don't! Many snakes will regurgitate their first meal if it's too big. After months of not eating, they need to build up to it. If *you* fasted for weeks and then went to an all-you-can eat restaurant and pigged-out, you might feel good at first, but I can guarantee you'll be sick later. Start the snakes out with a couple of hopper mice. Five or six days later, offer a couple of small adult mice. Only after that should you start feeding them large prey. Now feed them as much as they will eat for four or five weeks. At the end of this time they'll be feeling fine and ready for breeding.

There is no easy way to be sure if a male is fertile, but some breeders like to *palpate* a female before mating her. By gently pressing the belly toward the backbone for several inches above the anal plate, you should be able to feel some small "bumps"—these are ripe ovarian follicles. One follicle = one egg; some breeders have such a fine touch that they can reliably estimate clutch size before the female has even mated! If you don't feel the follicles it may be too early to mate this particular female. If you do feel some, however, it is all right to go ahead. Another good indicator of the female's breeding readiness is molting. Most females begin mating only after the first shed of the season.

Now is the time we've been waiting for. The usual procedure is to move the female to the male's cage, not the other way around. The rationale is that the female's cage is so impregnated with her scent that the male may become confused, so by introducing her to the male's cage he is immediately able to isolate her scent. The male will quickly become excited and will glide over to the female. He climbs on top of her and writhes all over her back. This dorsal stimulation apparently gets the female excited. This courtship can last only a few minutes but often goes on for several hours. Eventually the female, if she is receptive, will signal the male by raising her tail. The male wraps his tail around the females and everts his hemipenis, inserting one lobe of it into the female's cloaca. Sometimes this causes the female to tense up or even flee. If she does, the male is in a very uncomfortable position, as he cannot disengage very quickly. It may seem comical to everyone except the male in question, but it is not uncommon in many snake species for the female to slither off, dragging the male by his organ. To prevent this, the male may bite the female at the base of the neck to help keep her still and in a parallel position.

One copulation may be enough to get the female "pregnant" (*gravid* is the more correct term for egg-laying animals), but multiple matings will increase your odd's of getting a good percentage of fertile eggs. Three or four matings over the course of 2-4 weeks is a good number. Some breeders use the same male, and others use different males to reduce the odds of having infertile eggs because a particular male was a "dud." After each mating, return the female to her cage.

EGG-LAYING

The time from mating to egg-laying varies considerably, anywhere from six to 12 weeks.

During this period the female may nearly double in girth. It is important to feed her very heavily at this time. Up to four adult mice per week should be offered. As gestation progresses the female will have less room in her abdominal cavity for large food items because of the developing eggs. It is not unusual for her to stop feeding at this time, but you can probably prevent this from happening by switching to smaller, more frequent meals. Rat pups or hopper mice are particularly favored.

The female always sheds 6-14 days before laying her eggs; this will probably be her second post-brumation molt. When you notice this molt, it's time to provide a nesting box of some sort. A plastic shoebox or large plastic salad container with a 2-inch-diameter hole cut in the lid will work fine. It should be half-filled with damp vermiculite, sphagnum moss, or sterile sand. The vermiculite is probably the best medium, but each breeder has his preference. Place the nest box at the cool end of the cage's thermal gradient

The female will become increasingly restless and will spend more and more time inside the nest box. Then, she should suddenly settle down and spend virtually all of her time inside the nest box. You may be fortunate enough to catch the female in the act of laying her eggs, but it often happens at night, so don't be too surprised if you don't. As soon as you are sure she is finished laying (no new eggs appear for at least several hours), you can very gently remove the female (she will be very tired) and place her in a darkened, quiet cage by herself. Offer plenty of water but do not attempt to feed her for at least a day. Alternatively, some breeders leave her with the eggs for 24 hours before removing her. She does not guard the eggs in any way, but these breeders feel that allowing her to recoup some small measure of her strength before being moved is desirable.

The number of eggs laid is remarkably variable, which should not be surprising, because there are lots of variables involved. The snake's age, weight, overall health, and fat/calcium stores are all involved. Anywhere from 3-24 eggs have been recorded from Cal Kings. They are leathery and about 2 inches long.

You should probably allow your pair of snakes to mate a few times to ensure high fertility. This is a pair of Nuevo Leon Kingsnakes, *L. mexicana thayeri,* caught in the act. Photo by I. Francais.

DOUBLE CLUTCHING

Often it is not difficult to induce female Cal Kings to *double clutch*; that is, lay two separate batches of eggs in the same breeding season. If you wish to do this, it should be only with large, robust females at least several years old. It may be overly stressful on a first-time breeder.

Preparation for double clutching should begin even before the female has laid her first clutch of eggs. We discussed the importance of reducing prey size when a female's eggs are ripening, and this will also help you when trying to get females to double clutch. Females that do not go on a hunger strike before depositing their first batch of eggs are more likely to have the energy reserves to support the development of a second clutch.

Regardless of whether she has eaten or not, after she has laid her first clutch you want to feed the female as much as she will eat. Offer a good-sized mouse every day if she will take it; even two on some days if she is up to it.

Kingsnakes are not known to store sperm as some reptiles can, using it to fertilize multiple clutches of eggs. If she is to double clutch, the female must be placed with a male within two weeks after she has laid the first clutch. Really, you should do it as soon as possible; as soon as the females no longer looks tired from the ordeal of laying the first batch. This can often be within three to four days. If you go beyond two weeks, she may have

a post-egg-laying molt, and for some reason females that are mated after this molt rarely have a second clutch that season.

Second clutches are normally smaller than the first, both in number and in the size of the individual eggs, but the hatchlings resulting are every bit as viable as those from first clutches.

INCUBATION

As soon as you have removed the female from the nesting box, it is time to remove the eggs to an incubator that has been set to keep a steady temperature of 82°F, give or take a couple of degrees (but no more!). They should be placed individually with the same side up as they were laid, about 2 inches apart, half buried in a bed of moist vermiculite. Most breeders prefer about a 1:1 ratio of water to vermiculite (by weight, not volume), but some prefer it just a little bit drier. The vermiculite should be distinctly damp to the touch but *not* wet. If the eggs are glued together as one big mass, do not attempt to separate them. They are fragile, and you risk tearing them. Simply space the eggs in a shallow depression in the vermiculite and hope for the best.

There are many different types of incubators. Some keepers use converted poultry incubators, some use ones designed especially for herp eggs, and other jury-rig some contraption of their own. A simple design that works well for small batches of eggs is to simply fill a 10-gallon aquarium halfway with water and place a 50-watt submersible aquarium heater in the water and adjust the temperature until it is in the correct range and holding steady. The eggs are placed in a plastic shoebox or a box of similar size and shape. The shoebox is covered with its own lid and then the whole thing is propped up on a couple of bricks so that the

No matter what sort of incubator you use, do yourself a favor and anticipate the need for it. It will take a couple of days to calibrate it, and it's not good to be trying to get it set up when the eggs have already arrived.

Check on the progress of the eggs at least every three to four days. Any eggs that are infertile will soon show themselves. Called "slugs" in herp breeder

Frequently, snakes will lay eggs when there are no observers, but once in a while breeders will get lucky and witness the laying. Here is an Albino Speckled Kingsnake laying her eggs. Photo by I. Francais.

water surface is about an inch below the bottom of the box. I have even floated the box on the water itself with good results. The tank opening is covered with a sheet of plastic wrap to keep the heat and humidity in. (An important tip: calibrate the temperature with the plastic wrap in place, or the temperature will rise after you cover it).

slang, they deflate and become yellowish-brown in color, and may exude foul-smelling decaying yolk. Remove them as soon as you're sure they are slugs, or they may contaminate nearby good eggs with bacteria or fungi.

Some breeders gently remove the eggs and replace all of the vermiculite about halfway through the incubation period. Others do not and usually still have good results as long as they keep close tabs on the eggs. Still, if you have the time, it couldn't hurt.

At 82°F, incubation of Cal King eggs takes about seven to ten weeks. The eggs may "deflate" slightly when very close to term; do not be alarmed. The babies "pip" the eggs several hours to a day before hatching, slicing a small opening with the egg tooth on the tip of the snout. This is lost several days after hatching. The babies may hatch within a few hours of each other, or may be staggered over the course of about two days. Do not attempt to help them hatch. You will probably do more harm than good. If they are healthy the babies will emerge from the eggs in their own time; any that do not were probably too weak to survive long beyond hatching anyway.

REARING YOUNG

New Cal King hatchlings are about 12 inches long. It is best if each one can be placed in its own small enclosure, as some cannibalism may occur when the babies are kept together. Pet shops sell "small animal cages" under various brand names; these are basically small plastic aquariums with slotted plastic lids that clip into place to prevent escape. I use them a lot for small herps. They are attractive, easy to clean, and almost escape-proof when used correctly. If you have bought just one snake to raise as a pet, it can go right into a 10-gallon tank, but beware of the size of the mesh in the cage's screen top. Unless they are well fed, young hatchlings could conceivably slip through the quarter-inch mesh of a standard screen top. There are, however, cage tops with eighth-inch mesh, so use these instead. Use paper toweling for the substrate, provide a water bowl no more than an inch deep and a couple of inches in diameter.

Like the cages in which adult snakes are kept, the babies' enclosures should have hideboxes and a thermal gradient. The latter can be created by heating pads or heat tape placed along the back of a shelf that contains a number of baby cages. Again, when using any heating device, be sure to use it according to the manufacturer's directions to ameliorate the risk of fire or of overheating your snakes. Some sort of thermostat is a must.

The hatchlings probably will not feed until after their first shed, about a week after hatching. They should be offered thawed frozen newborn pinkies, perhaps wiggled a bit with long forceps to entice the baby snakes into striking. Most will feed. A few will need to be fed live newborn pinkies. A very few will still refuse to eat. These will often accept a frozen pinkie that has been washed, blotted dry, and rubbed on a small lizard such as an anole or house gecko. (You can use a live lizard, but they object strenuously. If possible, it's better to use a frozen one.) As a last resort, you can use the freshly broken and squirming tail of a house gecko. Any snakes that still refuse to feed can be very gently force-fed, and some of these will later learn to take food on their own. A few never feed, never will, and die in spite of anything you do. Don't despair. Some mortality is inevitable, but with good care and patience, the vast majority of your babies will survive.

The babies should be offered two to three pinkies a week at first, with the size increased proportionally as the babies grow. Food items should never be more than about 1.5 times the width of a snake's head.

HEALTH

With hygienic cage conditions and attention to basic case and maintenance, you should never need to refer to this chapter. That's why I named it "Health" and not "Illness"—to remind you that the emphasis in the care of pet snakes should be on selecting a healthy snake and never exposing it to diseases or predisposing stress that can cause sickness. That being said, below are a few of the many diseases and parasites that can afflict California Kingsnakes. It should be emphasized that many

Some keepers use plastic garbage cans to hold their snakes while cleaning the cages. Always disinfect temporary containers between occupants to prevent the spread of parasites and diseases. Photo by I. Francais.

disease conditions require exacting diagnosis and treatment for a successful resolution. In short, you should not hesitate to contact a veterinarian if you feel you're in over your head. Your pet shop, a local zoo, or a university with a herpetology department should be able to recommend someone in your area. It used to be hard to find a herp vet, but fortunately, many vets have become savvy to the fact that herps of all types are popular pets and that they can't ignore pets beyond dogs and cats.

MITES

Everybody hates mites. These eight-legged little pests are the bane of every herp-keeper, and every herp-keeper has had to deal with them at one time or another. They may be hard to see, especially because they are nocturnal and tend to stay concealed beneath the scales of their host by day, however, if you switch on the lights suddenly at night and see your snake with pinhead-sized brown or red dots crawling on it, you've got mites.

Getting rid of them is a two-pronged operation. You have to get them off the snake, and you have to sterilize the cage. Mites leave their host and lay their eggs somewhere in the cage. Bark or soil substrates are especially favorable to mites; sand and other dry substrates tend to desiccate them and their eggs.

First, the snake. There are pyrethrin-based sprays under a number of brand names. Most require that you spray the reptile

with it, leave it on for a minute or so, then rinse it off with tepid water. It's important to keep the stuff out of mouths, eyes, and nasal passages (yours and your snakes'). Pyrethrins are plant-based, naturally occurring toxins (found in chrysanthemums, among others), and are very toxic to mites and not *extremely* toxic to higher animals like you and your herps, but you should still handle them with care.

The cage must be sterilized with very hot water, perhaps with a tablespoon of bleach per gallon. Anything that can't be sterilized must be discarded. When the tank is well rinsed and dry again (there shouldn't be any trace of bleach odor), set it back up with paper toweling and a plastic hidebox. Give the inside of the cage two even spritzes of the mite spray and let dry for 15 minutes. Only now fill the water bowl and place it in the cage. And then put the now mite-free snake (we hope) into the cage. Repeat the treatment in another week, and keep the cage set up in this clinical fashion for at least a couple of weeks beyond that, or until you can be sure that the mites have not returned.

Another approach to dealing with mites is to cut a square of insecticidal "pest strip," about one inch square, and place it inside a perforated plastic pill bottle in a well-ventilated cage. Most pest strips currently on the market contain 2,2 dichlorovinyl dimethyl phosphate (also called dichlorvos). Organic toxins like this can be very effective but can also have some very nasty side effects when used incorrectly. I speak from experience. I can remember when I was a kid and used way too much pest strip on a mite-infested Desert Iguana. I killed the mites, but the lizard was never the same and suffered from tremors and seizures. Liver damage is also a possibility. Some herp keepers swear by pest strips, but if you opt for them, use small amounts, never forget that the cage must be well-ventilated, and remove it as soon as the mites are eradicated, which is rarely more that a week.

By the way, if mites weren't trouble enough, they travel easily. If you have mites in one cage in your setup, they're probably in every cage. They will literally walk out of one cage and travel to the other side of the room or sometimes another room entirely, infesting another cage and its occupants. Eternal vigilance and careful quarantine of newly arrived animals is the price you pay to keep mites in check.

SHEDDING PROBLEMS

Kingsnakes should be kept in dry cages, but sometimes the low humidity can lead to skin shedding problems, especially right after emergence from brumation. Instead of shedding the skin in one piece, the snake may shed in loose patches. Often, all it takes to correct the situation is to place a damp paper towel and the snake into an old cotton pillowcase, knotted at the open end. Keep the snake in a warm place to keep it from getting chilled while it is damp, and check on it in 24 hours.

It should have gotten rid of most of the loose skin, and the rest you can probably peel off gently with your fingers.

One special problem with molting problems occurs at the eyes. Snakes, as you'll recall, do not have movable eyelids, but a transparent scale called a brille, speculum, or simply eyecap. Sometimes a snake fails to shed the eyecap, which will have some ragged skin surrounding it. You can wait until the next shed, and sometimes the snake will manage to shed both layers with the next molt. On the other hand you can gently intervene. First you must use warm water or glycerin to soften the retained eyecap. Allow at least a half hour. Grasp the ragged skin at the edge of the eyecap and pull gently. There should be little resistance, and the old eyecap will lift off. If you have any doubt about what you're doing, take a trip to the vet instead of risking blinding your snake.

BLISTERS

Snakes kept on wet, soiled substrates often develop what herp keepers call "skin blister disease," which probably arises from a number of bacterial and fungal vectors. Treatment involves washing the snake and moving it to a warm, clean, dry cage. Daily swabbing with povidone-iodine will usually lead to remission over the course of several weeks.

MOUTH ROT

Sometimes Cal Kings will show an unusual amount of mucus buildup around the mouth.

Usually, swabbing the mouth with a little bit of povidone-iodine and warm water and then keeping the snake in a "clinical cage" for a while will work.

A far worse oral condition that may or may not be related to the above is "mouth rot," or the more technically correct term, *infectious stomatitis*. A cheesy-looking (caseous) material appears at the edges of the mouth. The gums are very tender and bleed easily. This is a highly contagious bacterial infection, and any snake with it must be immediately isolated. This is yet another good reason to keep kingsnakes and all other snakes individually—if there's ever a problem, the snake is already isolated.

With a cotton swab dipped in povidone-iodine (some keepers recommend mixing this with hydrogen peroxide), swab out the caseous material every day and rise with warm water and a weak solution of povidone-iodine. An eyedropper or syringe (sans needle) is useful for irrigating the mouth of an affected snake. If you catch mouth rot early and are persistent in treatment (progress may be slow), the prognosis is good.

Mouth rot is often a secondary infection of a mechanical injury, such as an abrasion from the snake striking the glass or rubbing its shout raw on the cage lid. Fine window-type screening should never be used for cage lids, as it is very abrasive if a snake takes to continually rubbing against it. Stick with eighth-inch or quarter-inch hardware cloth and you'll have much less incidence of this.

INTERNAL BACTERIAL INFECTIONS

Snakes kept under perennially substandard conditions, especially when their food is left laying in a soiled area, may become infected by several different types of bacteria, notably *Pseudomonas* and *Aeromonas* species. Wholesale mortality of hatchling kingsnakes often has one of these bacteria as an underlying cause. When confronted by such "anomalous" deaths, immediately get fecal samples to your vet for identification of the organism and prescription of the correct antibiotic(s). In the meantime, sterilize everything you can, isolate any snakes being kept communally, and make sure cage conditions are as sterile as possible. These bacteria are often devastatingly fast-moving in terms of their infection rates and lethality, so don't waste a minute!

If you've stuck with me all the way, thanks for reading this far. By now you have all the necessary knowledge to keep your California kingsnakes alive and healthy, and even to breed them someday if you wish. Regardless of your ultimate goals with them, however, you'll find them to be engaging, attractive, gentle pets you'll be proud to keep and display. They can live for over 20 years with good care, so your relationship with that hatchling you brought home from the pet shop today has every reason to be a long one. I hope this book will help. Good luck!